Evangelism for Every Day

A four-week course to help people share their faith in everyday situations.

by
Stephen Parolini

Apply·It·To·Life™

Adult

BIBLE CURRICULUM
from Group

Group
Loveland, Colorado

Group

Evangelism for Every Day
Copyright © 1995 Group Publishing, Inc.

This curriculum book is a significantly revised edition of a book by the same title. Copyright © 1993 Group Publishing, Inc., Box 481, Loveland, CO 80539.

All rights reserved. No part of this book may be reproduced in any manner whatsoever without prior written permission from the publisher, except where noted on handouts and in the case of brief quotations embodied in critical articles and reviews. For information, write Permissions, Group Publishing, Inc., Dept. BK, Box 481, Loveland, CO 80539.

Credits
Editors: Bob Buller and Paul Woods
Senior Editor: Paul Woods
Creative Products Director: Joani Schultz
Cover Designer: Liz Howe
Interior Designer: Kathy Benson
Cover Photographer: Liz Howe
Cover Illustrator: Jose Ortega; The Stock Illustration Source, Inc.
Illustrators: Kathy Benson and Rex Bohn

ISBN 1-55945-515-2

10 9 8 7 6 5 4 3 2 1   04 03 02 01 00 99 98 97 96 95

Printed in the United States of America.

C O N T E N T S

Know What You Believe
We can share our faith with confidence when we know what we believe.

Truth in Plain Language
It's important to speak in plain language when we tell others about Christ.

Actions Speak Louder
Our actions can be a powerful witness for Christ.

Gifted to Tell
We can use our unique gifts and abilities to teach others about Jesus.

Introduction

WHAT IS APPLY-IT-TO-LIFE™ ADULT BIBLE CURRICULUM?

Apply-It-To-Life™ Adult Bible Curriculum is a series of four-week study courses designed to help you facilitate powerful lessons that will help class members grow in faith. Use this course with
- Sunday school classes,
- home study groups,
- weekday Bible study groups,
- men's Bible studies,
- women's Bible studies, and
- family classes.

The variety of courses gives the adult student a broad coverage of topical, life-related issues and significant biblical topics. In addition, as the name of the series implies, every lesson helps the adult student apply Scripture to his or her life.

Each course in Apply-It-To-Life Adult Bible Curriculum provides four lessons on different aspects of one topic. In each course, you also receive Fellowship and Outreach Specials connected to the month's topic. They provide suggestions for building closer relationships in your class, outreach activities, and even a party idea!

WHAT MAKES APPLY-IT-TO-LIFE ADULT BIBLE CURRICULUM UNIQUE?

Teaching as Jesus Taught

Jesus was a master teacher. With Apply-It-To-Life Adult Bible Curriculum, you'll use the same teaching methods and principles that Jesus used:
- **Active Learning.** Think back on an important lesson you've learned in life. Did you learn it from reading about it? from hearing about it? from something you did? Chances are, the most important lessons you've learned

came from something you experienced. That's what active learning is—learning by doing. Active learning leads students through activities and experiences that help them understand important principles, messages, and ideas. It's a discovery process that helps people internalize and remember what they learn.

Jesus often used active learning. One of the most vivid examples is his washing of his disciples' feet. In Apply-It-To-Life Adult Bible Curriculum, the teacher might remove his or her shoes and socks then read aloud the foot-washing passage from John 13, or the teacher might choose to actually wash people's feet. Participants won't soon forget it. Active learning uses simple activities to teach profound lessons.

● **Interactive Learning.** Interactive learning means learning through small-group interaction and discussion. While it may seem to be a simple concept, it's radically new to many churches that have stuck with a lecture format or large-group discussion for so long. With interactive learning, each person is actively involved in discovering God's truth through talking with other people about God's Word. Interactive learning is discussion with a difference. It puts people in pairs, trios, or foursomes to involve everyone in the learning experience. It takes active learning a step further by having people who have gone through an experience teach others what they've learned.

Jesus often helped cement the learning from an experience by questioning people—sometimes in small groups—about what had happened. He regularly questioned his followers and his opponents, forcing them to think and to discuss among themselves what he was teaching them. After washing his disciples' feet, the first thing Jesus did was ask the disciples if they understood what he had done. After the "foot washing" activity, the teacher might form small groups and have people discuss how they felt when the leader removed his or her shoes and socks. Then group members could compare those feelings and the learning involved to what the disciples must have experienced.

● **Biblical Depth.** Apply-It-To-Life Adult Bible Curriculum recognizes that most people are ready to go below the surface to better understand the deeper truths of the Bible. Therefore, the activities and studies go beyond an "easy answer" approach to Christian education and lead people to grapple with difficult issues from a biblical perspective.

Each lesson begins by giving the teacher resource material on the Bible passages covered in the study. In the Bible Basis, you'll find information that will help you understand the Scriptures you're dealing with. Within the class-time section of the lesson, thought-provoking activities and discussions lead adults to new depths of biblical understanding. Bible Insights within the lesson give pertinent information that will bring the Bible to life for you and your class members. In-class handouts give adults significant Bible information and challenge them to search for and discover biblical truths for themselves. Finally, the "For Even Deeper Discussion" sections provide questions that will lead your class members to new and deeper levels of insight and application.

No one questions the depth of Jesus' teachings or the effectiveness of his teaching methods. This curriculum follows Jesus' example and helps people probe the depths of the Bible in a way no other adult curriculum does.

● **Bible Application.** Jesus didn't stop with helping people understand truth. For him, teaching took the learner beyond understanding to application. It wasn't enough that the rich young ruler knew all the right answers. Jesus wanted him to take action on what he knew. In the same way, Apply-It-To-Life Adult Bible Curriculum encourages a response in people's lives. That's why this curriculum is called "Apply-It-To-Life"! Depth of understanding means little if the truths of Scripture don't zing into people's hearts. Each lesson brings home one point and encourages people to consider the changes they might make in response.

● **One Purpose.** In each study, every activity works toward communicating and applying the same point. People may discover other new truths, but the study doesn't load them down with a mass of information. Sometimes less is more. When lessons try to teach too much, they often fail to teach anything. Even Jesus limited his teaching to what he felt people could really learn and apply (John 16:12). Apply-It-To-Life Adult Bible Curriculum makes sure that class members thoroughly understand and apply one point each week.

● **Variety.** People appreciate variety. Jesus constantly varied his teaching methods. One day he would have a serious discussion with his disciples about who he was and another day he'd baffle them by turning water into wine. What he didn't do was allow them to become bored with what he had to teach them.

Any kind of study can become less than exciting if the leader and students do everything the same way week after week. Apply-It-To-Life Adult Bible Curriculum varies activities and approaches to keep everyone's interest level high each week. In one class, you might have people in small groups "put themselves in the disciples' sandals" and experience something of the confusion of Jesus' death and resurrection. In another lesson, class members may experience problems in communication and examine how such problems can damage relationships.

To meet adults' varied needs, the courses cover a wide range of topics such as Jesus, knowing God's will, communication, taking faith to work, and highlights of Bible books. One month you may choose to study a family or personal faith issue; the next month you may cover a biblical topic such as the book of John.

● **Relevance.** People today want to know how to live successfully right now. They struggle with living as authentic Christians at work, in the family, and in the community. Most churchgoing adults want to learn about the Bible, but not merely for the sake of having greater Bible knowledge. They want to know how the Bible can help them live faithful lives—how it can help them face the difficulties of living in today's culture. Apply-It-To-Life Adult Bible Curriculum bridges the gap between biblical truth and the "real world" issues of people's lives. Jesus didn't discuss with his followers the eschatological significance of Ezekiel's wheels, and Apply-It-To-Life Adult Bible Curriculum won't either! Courses and studies in this curriculum focus on the real needs of people and help them discover answers in Scripture that will help meet those needs.

● **A Nonthreatening Atmosphere.** In many adult classes, people feel intimidated because they're new Christians or because they don't have the Bible knowledge they think they should have. Jesus sometimes intimidated those who opposed him, but he consistently treated his followers with understanding and respect. We want people in church to experience the same understanding and respect Jesus' followers experienced. With Apply-It-To-Life Adult Bible Curriculum, no one is embarrassed for not knowing or understanding as much as someone else. In fact, the interactive learning process minimizes the differences between those with vast Bible knowledge and those with little Bible knowledge. Lessons often begin with nonthreatening, sharing questions and move slowly toward more depth. Whatever their level of knowledge or commitment, class members will work together to discover biblical truths that can affect their lives.

● **A Group That Cares.** Jesus began his ministry by choosing a group of 12 people who learned from him together. That group practically lived together—sharing one another's hurts, joys, and ambitions. Sometimes Jesus divided the 12 into smaller groups and worked with just three or four at a time.

Studies have shown that many adults today long for a close-knit group of people with whom they can share personal needs and joys. And people interact more freely when they feel accepted in a group. Activities in this curriculum will help class members get to know one another better and care for one another more as they study the Bible and apply its truths to their lives. As people reveal their thoughts and feelings to one another, they'll grow closer and develop more commitment to the group and to each other. And they'll be encouraging one another along the way!

● **An Element of Delight.** We don't often think about Jesus' ministry in this way, but there certainly were times he brought fun and delight to his followers. Remember the time he raised Peter's mother-in-law? or the time he sat happily with children on his lap? How about the joy and excitement at his triumphal entry into Jerusalem? or the time he helped fishing disciples catch a boatload of fish—after they'd fished all night with no success?

People learn more when they're having fun. So within Apply-It-To-Life Adult Bible Curriculum, elements of fun and delight pop up often. And sometimes adding fun is as simple as using a carrot for a pretend microphone!

Taking the Fear out of Teaching

Teachers love Apply-It-To-Life Adult Bible Curriculum because it makes teaching much less stressful. Lessons in this curriculum

● **are easy to teach.** Interactive learning frees the teacher from being a dispenser of information to serve as a facilitator of learning. Teachers can spend class time guiding people to discover and apply biblical truths. The studies provide clear, understandable Bible background; easy-to-prepare learning experiences; and powerful, thought-provoking discussion questions.

● **can be prepared quickly.** Lessons in Apply-It-To-Life Adult Bible Curriculum are logical and clear. There's no sorting through tons of information to figure out the lesson. In 30 minutes, a busy teacher can easily read a lesson and prepare to teach it. In addition, optional and For Extra Time activities allow the teacher to tailor the lesson to the class. And the thorough instructions and questions will guide even an inexperienced teacher through each powerful lesson.

● **let everyone share in the class's success.** With Apply-It-To-Life Adult Bible Curriculum, the teacher is one of the participants. The teacher still guides the class, but the burden is not as heavy. Everyone participates and adds to the study's effectiveness. So when the study has an impact, everyone shares in that success.

● **lead the teacher to new discoveries.** Each lesson is designed to help the teacher first discover a biblical truth. And most teachers will make additional discoveries as they prepare each lesson. In class, the teacher will discover even more as other adults share what they have found. As with any type of teaching, the teacher will likely learn more than anyone else in the class!

● **provide relevant information to class members.** Photocopiable handouts are designed to help people better understand or interpret Bible passages. And the handouts make teaching easier because the teacher can often refer to them for small-group discussion questions and instructions.

HOW TO USE APPLY-IT-TO-LIFE ADULT BIBLE CURRICULUM

First familiarize yourself with an Apply-It-To-Life Adult Bible Curriculum lesson. The following explanations will help you understand how the lesson elements work together.

Lesson Elements

● The **Opening** maps out the lesson's agenda and introduces your class to the topic for the session. Sometimes this activity will help people get better acquainted as they begin to explore the topic together.

● The **Bible Exploration and Application** activities will help people discover what the Bible says about the topic and how the lesson's point applies to their lives. In these varied activities, class members find answers to the "So what?" question. Through active and interactive learning methods, people will discover the relevance of the Scriptures and commit to growing closer to God.

You may use either one or both of the options in this section. They are designed to stand alone or to work together. Both present the same point in different ways. "For Even Deeper Discussion" questions appear at the end of each activity in this section. Use these questions whenever you feel they might be particularly helpful for your class.

● The **Closing** pulls everything in the lesson together and often funnels the lesson's message into a time of reflection and prayer.

● The **For Extra Time** section is just that. Use it when you've completed the lesson and still have time left or when you've used one Bible Exploration and Application option and don't have time to do the other. Or you might plan to use it instead of another option.

When you put all the sections together, you get a lesson that's fun and easy to teach. Plus, participants will learn truths they'll remember and apply to their daily lives.

About the Questions and Answers . . .

The answers given after discussion questions are responses participants *might* give. They aren't the only answers or the "right" answers. However, you can use them to spark discussion.

Real life doesn't always allow us to give the "right" answers. That's why some of the responses given are negative or controversial. If someone responds negatively, don't be shocked. Accept the person and use the opportunity to explore other perspectives on the issue.

To get more out of your discussions, use follow-up inquiries such as

- Tell me more.
- What do you mean by that?
- What makes you feel that way?

Guidelines for a Successful Adult Class

● **Be a facilitator, not a lecturer.** Apply-It-To-Life Adult Bible Curriculum is student-based rather than teacher-based. Your job is to direct the activities and facilitate the discussions. You become a choreographer of sorts: someone who gets everyone else involved in the discussion and keeps the discussion on track.

● **Teach adults how to form small groups.** Help adults discover the benefits of small-group discussions by assisting them in forming groups of four, three, or two—whatever the activity calls for. Small-group sharing allows for more discussion and involvement by all participants. It's not as threatening or scary to open up to two people as it would be to 20 or 200!

Some leaders decide not to form small groups because they want to hear everybody's ideas. The intention is good, but some people just won't talk in a large group. Use a "report back" time after small-group discussions to gather the best responses from all groups.

When you form small groups, don't always let people choose those right around them. Try creative group-forming methods to help everyone in the class get to know one another. For example, have class members form groups with others who are wearing the same color, are interested in the same kind of music, shop at the same grocery store, were born the same month, like the same sports team, or like the same season of the year. If you have fun with it, your class will, too!

● **Encourage relationship building.** George Barna, in his insightful book about the church, *The Frog in the Kettle,* explains that adults today have a strong need to develop friendships. In a society of high-tech toys, "personal" computers, and lonely commutes, people long for positive human contact. That's where our church classes and groups can jump in. Help adults form friendships through your class. What's discovered in a classroom setting will be better applied when friends support each other outside the classroom. In fact, the relationships begun in your class may be as important as the truths you help your adults learn.

● **Be flexible.** Sometimes your class will complete every activity in the lesson with great success and wonderful learning. But what should you do if people go off on a tangent? or they get stuck in one of the activities? What if you don't have time to finish the lesson?

Don't panic. People learn best when they are interested and engaged in meaningful discussion, when they move at their own pace. And if you get through even one activity, your class will discover the point for the whole lesson. So relax. It's OK if you don't get everything done. Try to get to the Closing in every lesson, since its purpose is to bring closure to the topic for the week. But if you don't, don't sweat it!

● **Expect the unexpected.** Active learning is an adventure that doesn't always take you where you think you're going. Don't be surprised if things don't go exactly the way you'd planned. Be open to the different directions the Holy Spirit may lead your class. When something goes wrong or an unexpected emotion is aroused, take advantage of this teachable moment. Ask probing questions; follow up on someone's deep need or concern. Those moments are often the best opportunities for learning that come our way.

● **Participate—and encourage participation.** Apply-It-To-Life Adult Bible Curriculum is only as interactive as you and your class make it. Learning arises out of dialogue. People need to grapple with and verbalize their questions and discoveries. Jump into discussions yourself, but don't "take over." Encourage everyone to participate. You can facilitate smooth discussions by using "active listening" responses such as rephrasing and summing up what's been said. If people seem stumped, use the possible responses after each question to spark further discussion. You may feel like a cheerleader at times, but your efforts will be worth it. The more people participate, the more they'll discover God's truths for themselves.

● **Trust the Holy Spirit.** All the previous six guidelines and the instructions in the lessons will be irrelevant if you ignore the presence of God in your classroom. God sent the Holy Spirit as our helper. As you use this curriculum, ask the Holy Spirit to help you facilitate the lessons. And ask the Holy Spirit to direct your class toward God's truth. Trust that God's Spirit can work through each person's discoveries, not just the teacher's.

How to Use This Course

Before the Four-Week Session
● Read the Course Introduction and This Course at a Glance (pp. 14-15).

● Decide how you'll use the art on the Publicity Page (p. 16) to publicize the course. Prepare fliers, newsletter articles, and posters as needed.

● Look at the Fellowship and Outreach Specials (pp. 63-64) and decide which ones you'll use.

Before Each Lesson
● Read the one-sentence Point, the Objectives, and the Bible Basis for the lesson. The Bible Basis provides background information on the lesson's passages and shows how those passages relate to people today.

● Choose which activities you'll use from the lesson. Remember, it's not important to do every activity. Pick the ones that best fit your group and time allotment.

● Gather necessary supplies. They're listed in This Lesson at a Glance.

● Read each section of the lesson. Adjust activities as necessary to fit your class size and meeting room, but be careful not to delete all the activity. People learn best when they're actively involved in the learning process.

People today want and need a personal relationship with a loving God, and it's our job to tell them how. But the days of street-corner and tent-meeting evangelism are waning, and Christians are looking for new ways to share their faith. Few people can preach the gospel to millions the way Billy Graham has, nor are most Christians called into professional ministry.

So how do we do it? How do regular, everyday people share their faith in Christ? Simple—we become evangelists for every day.

When Christ gave the Great Commission to his disciples (Matthew 28:18-20), he also gave their successors the same command: to share God's love with the world. Because we're the successors, it's our job to tell others about God's love.

By focusing on what we know about God's love, we can effectively speak to others about Christ's sacrifice on the cross. Also, when we speak in language that's free of the Christian jargon that confuses non-Christians (and separates churches), we can help others understand some of the important truths of our faith. Finally, when we pattern our lives after Christ, our actions can speak loudly about what it means to be a Christian.

This course will help adults discover ways to be evangelists in everyday situations—at work, at home, and among strangers. It will help them see that preaching from a soapbox, going door to door to invite people to church, and handing out tracts in shopping centers aren't the only (or even the best) ways to spread the gospel. As a result, it will help them discover how they can use their unique gifts to reach others with God's love.

This Course at a Glance

Before you dive into the lessons, familiarize yourself with each lesson's point. Then read the Scripture passages.

- Study them as a background to the lessons.
- Use them as a basis for your personal devotions.
- Think about how they relate to people's situations today.

Lesson 1: Know What You Believe
The Point: We can share our faith with confidence when we know what we believe.
Bible Basis: 1 Corinthians 15:1-11

Lesson 2: Truth in Plain Language
The Point: It's important to speak in plain language when we tell others about Christ.
Bible Basis: Acts 8:26-39 and 17:22-34

Lesson 3: Actions Speak Louder
The Point: Our actions can be a powerful witness for Christ.
Bible Basis: Philippians 2:1-5; Titus 2:7-8; and James 2:14-26

Lesson 4: Gifted to Tell
The Point: We can use our unique gifts and abilities to teach others about Jesus.
Bible Basis: Matthew 28:18-20; 2 Timothy 1:5-11; and 1 Peter 4:7-11

Grab your congregation's attention! Add the vital details to the ready-made flier below, photocopy it, and use it to advertise this course on evangelism for every day. Insert the flier in your bulletins. Enlarge it to make posters. Splash the art or anything else from this page in newsletters, bulletins, or even on postcards! It's that simple.

*The art from this page is also available on Group's MinistryNet™ computer on-line resource for you to manipulate on your computer. Call **800-447-1070** for information.*

EVANGELISM FOR EVERY DAY

A four-week adult course on sharing your faith in everyday circumstances.

COME TO

ON

AT

COME EXPLORE HOW YOU CAN SHARE GOD'S LOVE AND YOUR FAITH WITH CONFIDENCE.

Permission to photocopy this page granted for local church use. Copyright © Group Publishing, Inc., Box 481, Loveland, CO 80539.

Know What You Believe

We can share our faith with confidence when we know what we believe.

◀ **T H E   P O I N T**

OBJECTIVES

Participants will
- study 1 Corinthians 15:1-11 to discover the essentials of the Christian faith,
- identify their personal beliefs on significant theological issues, and
- determine what's important to know about the Christian faith when telling someone about Christ.

BIBLE BASIS

Look up the Scripture for this lesson. Then read the following background paragraphs to see how the passage relates to people today.

In **1 Corinthians 15:1-11,** Paul defends belief in the idea of a bodily resurrection.

1 CORINTHIANS 15:1-11

The Corinthian church was plagued by a number of moral and theological problems. For example, many Corinthians had adopted a dualistic worldview that regarded everything physical as evil and everything spiritual as good. To accommodate this new perspective, the Corinthians had to redefine the doctrine of resurrection. They didn't deny resurrection per se, but they replaced the idea of *bodily* resurrection with belief in the *spiritual* resurrection of the human soul. Paul wrote 1 Corinthians 15 to correct their faulty worldview and to defend the Christian teaching that everyone who dies will be raised bodily from the grave.

BIBLE INSIGHT

The statement that Christ "died for our sins" probably implies two things. First, Christ's death atoned or paid the penalty for our sins. Second, Christ's death was a substitution for our own deserved deaths. In short, Christ died on our behalf and in our place.

Paul states his purpose in verses 1-2. He's going to remind the Corinthians of the gospel he had preached and they had received. He wants to demonstrate that their adherence to the gospel is vain if their interpretation of it (without death and bodily resurrection) is correct. In so doing, he hopes to restore them to the true gospel—the gospel that has the power to save them.

Paul reminds them of the gospel by reciting the earliest known Christian creed or summary of beliefs (verses 3b-5). The creed lists four foundational beliefs of the Christian faith:

- Christ died for our sins.
- Christ was buried.
- Christ was raised to life on the third day.
- Christ appeared to Peter and the other disciples.

Paul uses this creed to prove to the Corinthians that, just as Jesus Christ *physically* died and was buried, he was *physically* raised and appeared to reliable witnesses. Moreover, because Christ died and was raised *physically,* other people will also die and be raised *physically.* The Corinthians can deny the latter only by rejecting the heart of the gospel, which is founded on the physical death, burial, resurrection, and post-resurrection appearance of Jesus Christ.

Paul supplements the creed (and strengthens his argument) by listing additional witnesses who saw Jesus Christ with their own eyes after his resurrection and by stating that even he has seen the risen Christ (verses 6-8). Finally, Paul tells the Corinthians that, although he may be the least of the apostles in terms of length of service, all the apostles teach the same gospel (verses 9-11). Therefore, the Corinthians must not compromise the gospel Paul taught them. On the contrary, they need to renounce their faulty worldview and reaffirm their commitment to the true gospel, which is based on the sacrificial death, burial, and physical resurrection of Jesus Christ.

Few people would be confident enough to tell someone how to program a computer if they barely knew how to do it themselves. In the same way, Christians who have only a sketchy understanding of the Christian faith are unlikely to have the confidence to tell others about their relationship with God. In addition, Christians who don't know the basics of their faith will be like the Corinthians, subject to the damaging influence of whatever false ideas come their way. Use this lesson to help your class members affirm and understand the basics of the Christian faith. Not only will they be better able to avoid modern perversions of the gospel, they'll also possess the confidence to tell others about their faith.

Section	Minutes	What Participants Will Do	Supplies
OPENING	*up to 10*	**FAITH STORIES**—Share stories of how they became Christians.	
BIBLE EXPLORATION AND APPLICATION	*25 to 30*	☐ *Option 1:* **WHAT ARE THE BASICS?**—Discuss how to sell a make-believe object, then study 1 Corinthians 15:1-11 to discover basic beliefs of the Christian faith.	Bibles, "What's Important?" handouts (p. 26), paper, pencils, newsprint, marker
	20 to 25	☐ *Option 2:* **CRITICAL ISSUES**—Determine theological issues critical to their faith.	Bibles, "Critical Issues" handouts (p. 27), pencils
CLOSING	*up to 10*	**HELP ME TO KNOW YOU**—Pray that God will give them confidence in reaching out to others.	
FOR EXTRA TIME	*up to 10*	**OTHER CREEDS**—Evaluate their church or denominational statement of faith.	
	up to 10	**TALK TO ME**—Practice explaining their faith to partners.	
	up to 10	**BIG QUESTIONS**—List and begin to answer their biggest questions about the Christian faith.	Concordances, Bible encyclopedias

TIP

People have wonderfully varied
faith stories. Remind everyone that
some stories will be dramatic and
dynamic ("I was rescued from
drugs," or "I was an atheist until I
saw a vision of Christ"). Others will
be quiet and subtle ("I was raised
in a Christian home," or "My faith
journey began as a child, and I'm
still on the road"). Both kinds of
faith stories are equally valid and
help us discover the incredible
diversity and creativity of our faith.

If some class members don't wish to
tell their stories, allow them to pass
or tell about a friend's faith journey.

OPENING

Faith Stories

(up to 10 minutes)

As you begin class, thank class members for attending and tell them what they'll be discussing in today's lesson. Use the following statement or your own summary of the main point: **Welcome to the first week of our study on evangelism. During the next four weeks, we're going to explore how we can follow Christ's commandment to tell others about God and his love for them. Not everyone is a skilled preacher or what we often call an "evangelist," but anyone can learn how to tell others about Jesus. Even now we can share our own faith stories with others.**

Form groups of four or fewer. Have people each take one or two minutes to tell their groups how they became Christians.

After everyone has shared, ask for volunteers to tell the rest of the class some of their group members' stories. As much as possible, emphasize the diversity of experiences in the class. Then have group members discuss the following questions. Ask:

● **What similarities are there in these faith stories?** (We all felt the need to reach out to God; God used other people to help us discover Christ.)

● **What roles did other Christians play in your faith journey?** (They helped me see my need for a personal relationship with Jesus; they showed me by example how wonderful it is to be a Christian.)

Say: **Whether it's a father who prays with his children or a friend who presents the Christian life by example, Christians can have a powerful influence on non-Christians.** ▷ **However, to share our faith with confidence we need to know what we believe. That's where we'll begin today.**

THE POINT ▷

BIBLE EXPLORATION AND APPLICATION

☐ OPTION 1:

What Are the Basics?

(25 to 30 minutes)

Before class, make one photocopy of the "What's Important?" handout (p. 26) for each person in the class.

Keep people in groups of four. Give each group a sheet of paper and a pencil.

Say: **I want you to imagine that I've just invented**

an incredible new device called a frabbistat, and you're going to help me sell it. In your group, draw a picture of a frabbistat and list any questions that potential buyers might ask about it. In five minutes, we'll compare our drawings and questions.

Don't answer any questions about the frabbistat (because there really is no such thing). After five minutes, ask groups to display their drawings and read their questions to the rest of the class. Then have group members discuss the following questions. After each question, ask for volunteers to report their groups' insights. Ask:

● **How easy was it to draw the frabbistat? to create a list of questions? Explain.** (It was hard because we didn't know where to begin; it was difficult because each of us had a different idea about what it should look like.)

● **When is explaining your Christian beliefs like trying to sell a frabbistat? When is it different?** (It's similar when we don't know what we're talking about; it's similar if we're talking to someone who doesn't believe that God exists; it's easier to share our faith when the other person wants a relationship with God.)

● **How are your questions similar to questions non-Christians ask about Christianity? How are they different?** (Both are vague and unclear; both reflect a high degree of confusion; the questions non-Christians ask deserve thoughtful answers.)

● **What kinds of questions do non-Christians often ask about Christianity?** (Why should I become a Christian? How can a loving God let innocent people suffer? What makes Jesus different from everyone else? Isn't sincerity of belief more important than what a person believes?)

As groups report the questions non-Christians often ask, write them on a sheet of newsprint. Then hang the newsprint where everyone can see it so you can refer to these questions later in this activity.

Say: **Because no one really knows what a frabbistat is, it would be difficult to sell one to someone who asked all the questions you listed. In the same way, it's hard to tell others about becoming a Christian when we don't know what that means or when we feel as though we have to answer all the questions they might ask. However, the essential beliefs of the Christian faith are really quite simple. Paul summarizes them for us in 1 Corinthians 15:1-11.**

Give a copy of the "What's Important?" handout to everyone and a pencil to anyone who needs one. Have people carry out the instructions at the top of the handout and then discuss the handout questions with their group members.

Several clues indicate that Paul is using an already-existing creed in 1 Corinthians 15:3b-5. First, he says he "handed on" (Greek: *paradidōmi*) what he had "received" (Greek: *paralambanō*). Both words are technical terms that refer to the passing on of a fixed tradition. Second, these verses contain many phrases and words Paul didn't normally use: "for our sins," "according to the Scriptures," "buried," "was raised," "the third day," and "the Twelve." In sum, 1 Corinthians 15:1-11 is probably the earliest summary of the Christian faith we have.

T H E P O I N T ▷

T E A C H E R
TIP

If you prefer, have people rate the importance of the questions on a scale of 1 to 10, with 1 representing "not at all important" and 10 representing "extremely important."

After approximately 10 minutes, have groups summarize their conclusions for the rest of the class. Then instruct group members to discuss the following questions. After each question, ask for volunteers to report their groups' answers to the rest of the class. Ask:

● **What do you think of Paul's summary of the Christian faith?** (Everything he listed is essential; we still need to explain many of the things he described; it's brief enough to easily learn.)

● **Should we add any other beliefs to the ones Paul listed? If so, which ones?** (Yes, we need to mention Jesus' deity; yes, we should add something about the necessity of faith in Jesus; no, Paul lists all the basics.)

● **Let's evaluate the questions on the newsprint on the basis of what we've discussed. Which questions are most important? Which are least important? Explain.** Answers will vary.

● **How can Paul's summary in 1 Corinthians 15 help you explain your faith with confidence?** (I can memorize the main points; I can study all the points so I can explain them clearly; I can build on it to create my own statement of faith.)

Say: **If we had to know all the answers before we could share our faith, we'd never open our mouths. Fortunately,▷ we can share our faith with confidence when we know the simple truths of what we believe. Take your handout home and review it from time to time so you'll be ready to explain what a Christian believes the next time you're asked.**

■■■■■■■■■■■■■■■■■■■■■■■■■■■■■
FOR *Even Deeper*
DISCUSSION

Form groups of four or fewer and discuss the following questions:

● Can a person become a Christian without believing all the statements Paul lists in 1 Corinthians 15:3b-5? Does believing that Paul's statements are true make a person a Christian? What's the difference between believing that the gospel is true and trusting Jesus for the gift of eternal life?

● Are there any elements of the Christian faith that cannot be explained? If so, what are they? How should we respond when a non-Christian asks us to explain one of these beliefs?
■■■■■■■■■■■■■■■■■■■■■■■■■■■■■

□ OPTION 2:
Critical Issues
(20 to 25 minutes)

Before class, make one copy of the "Critical Issues" handout (p. 27) for each class member.

Give each person a copy of the "Critical Issues" handout and a pencil. Say: **Few people have the time and resources to explore every aspect of the Christian faith, so it's important for us to know what's really vital to our faith. Take the next five minutes to complete the handout, then choose a partner to discuss the questions at the bottom of the handout. Be honest about your beliefs and sensitive to others' beliefs as you discuss these issues.**

After five minutes, encourage everyone to finish the handout and find a partner to discuss the questions at the bottom of the handout. Allow five minutes for discussion, then ask people to report which statements they marked "essential." Encourage participants to discuss areas of disagreement so they can understand each other as fully as possible. Then have each pair join another pair to form a group of four. Instruct groups to read **1 Corinthians 15:1-11** and to discuss the following questions. Ask for volunteers to report their groups' answers after each question. Ask:

● **What do our responses on this handout reveal about the issues that are important to us?** (We all agree on the essentials of the faith; we think a lot of issues are important; we have a short list of necessary beliefs.)

● **How is our list of important beliefs similar to Paul's? How is it different?** (We both put the most importance on our beliefs about Jesus; we both have only a few essential beliefs; we require a lot more than Paul does.)

● **What could we do to make our list more like Paul's? to better understand the beliefs Paul listed?** (We could re-evaluate what we think is really important; we could focus on the central issues of the faith instead of the peripheral issues.)

● **What would be the benefits of understanding more fully the beliefs Paul listed?** (We wouldn't get nervous when people ask us to explain the basics of the Christian faith; we'd appreciate what God has done for us even more; we wouldn't be easily confused by false teachers.)

Say: **Recognizing what's most important about the Christian faith makes it easier for us to know what we need to believe, and▷ knowing what we believe allows us to share our faith with confidence. We'll never have all the answers, but we can know enough of the answers to explain our faith clearly the next time someone asks.**

TEACHER TIP

To help people see how class members marked the statements, write the numerals 1-13 on a sheet of newsprint and hang it where everyone can see it. Then, as you read each statement, make a hash mark for everyone who marked that statement "essential."

◀ **THE POINT**

■■■■■■■■■■■■■■■■■■■■■■■■■■■■■■■■

FOR *Even Deeper*
DISCUSSION

Form groups of four or fewer and discuss the following questions:

● Should church or denominational statements of faith include every belief? only the essentials? some other combination? How can we use statements of faith positively? How do we sometimes use them negatively?

● Paul claims he worked harder than any other apostle but that it was God's grace working in him (1 Corinthians 15:10). What is the relation between our efforts and God's grace when we share our faith with others? In practical terms, how can we balance the two?

■■■■■■■■■■■■■■■■■■■■■■■■■■■■■■■

The "Apply-It-To-Life This Week" handout (p. 28) helps people further explore the issues uncovered in today's class. Give everyone a photocopy of the handout. Encourage class members to take time during the coming week to explore the questions and activities listed on the handout.

CLOSING

Help Me to Know You

(up to 10 minutes)

Say: **Telling someone about your faith in Christ is more than simply saying the right words. During the upcoming classes, we'll explore how to speak out of our faith experience, put our faith into practice, and develop our own styles of sharing Christ's love. Because this is a journey we'll take together, use the next few minutes to tell your group members what would give you more confidence when you share your faith. After everyone has shared, pray for each other, asking God to help each person develop the confidence to share his or her faith. When everyone's finished, we'll close together in prayer.**

After groups have prayed, form a circle. Say: **Think of someone you know who's not a Christian. You might think of a co-worker, a relative, or a friend.** Pause. **I'll open our prayer, then pause for people to call out the names of people they're thinking of. If you don't want to mention the name, you might call out "my friend" or say the name silently to God. I'll close the prayer when everyone who wants to has called out a name.**

Open the prayer with: **God, thank you for sending your Son to bring us eternal life.** ▷ **Help us understand what we believe so we can confidently reach out to those who don't yet know you...**

After the last name has been spoken, close the prayer and dismiss the class.

Thank adults for participating and encourage them to use the "Apply-It-To-Life This Week" handout during the coming week.

 For Extra Time

OTHER CREEDS
(up to 10 minutes)

Form groups of four or fewer. Give each group a copy of your denominational or church statement of faith. (If you prefer, distribute some other creed or statement of faith.) Instruct groups to evaluate the statement according to the categories given on the "Critical Issues" handout (p. 27). After groups evaluate the statement, direct groups to compare their conclusions and discuss any areas of disagreement. Then have groups discuss how to distinguish between the essentials and nonessentials of the Christian faith.

TALK TO ME
(up to 10 minutes)

Form pairs. Have people take turns explaining to each other their belief in Jesus Christ. Encourage everyone to ask thoughtful questions that might challenge the other person. Then have partners share with the whole group their ideas for dealing with difficult issues.

BIG QUESTIONS
(up to 10 minutes)

Ask people to call out or write their biggest questions about the Christian faith. Then form small groups to explore these questions. Provide Bible study tools such as concordances or Bible encyclopedias. Remind groups that it's OK if they don't find an answer today. Groups can spend several weeks discovering the answers to their questions. Address any unanswered questions to your pastor or someone else knowledgeable about Scripture and your church's specific beliefs.

■WHAT'S IMPORTANT?

Read 1 Corinthians 15:1-11 and the information in the FYI box. Then discuss the following questions with your group members. If necessary, consult the verses listed after each question.

1. Why is it important to believe that Christ died for our sins? (See also Romans 3:23-26.)

2. Why is it important to believe that Christ was buried? (See also Matthew 27:62-66.)

3. Why is it important to believe that Christ was raised on the third day? (See also 1 Corinthians 15:13-19.)

 Most biblical scholars agree that 1 Corinthians 15:3b-5 is the earliest creed or summary of Christian beliefs contained in the Bible. Because Paul says he "received" this summary of the gospel, it's probably a well-known statement of the gospel preached by the early church. No one knows when Paul received the creed—it may have been as early as 35 A.D. (Acts 11:25-30)—but it's clear that Paul regards this statement of the gospel "as of first importance" (1 Corinthians 15:3, NIV).

4. Why is it important to believe that Christ appeared to Peter and many others? (See John 20:19-29.)

Permission to photocopy this handout from Group's Apply-It-To-Life™ Adult Bible Curriculum granted for local church use.
Copyright © Group Publishing, Inc., Box 481, Loveland, CO 80539.

CRITICAL ISSUES

Read the statements below and mark whether you think a person needs to believe them to be a Christian. If, in your opinion, a person must believe a particular statement in order to be a Christian, mark the "essential" box. If a statement is important but not absolutely necessary, mark the "important" box. If a statement is true but not crucial to your faith, mark the "not important" box. Finally, if you don't believe that a statement is true, mark the "not true" box.

When you've marked all the statements, find a partner and discuss the questions at the bottom of the handout.

Yes! No! ???

	Essential	Important	Not Important	Not true
1. Jesus is God's Son.	❑	❑	❑	❑
2. The Bible is the unerring Word of God.	❑	❑	❑	❑
3. Jonah was swallowed by a large fish.	❑	❑	❑	❑
4. God will bless those who love him.	❑	❑	❑	❑
5. Jesus walked on water.	❑	❑	❑	❑
6. Jesus died on the cross.	❑	❑	❑	❑
7. The Bible has the answers to all of life's questions.	❑	❑	❑	❑
8. Jesus rose from the dead.	❑	❑	❑	❑
9. Jesus turned water into wine.	❑	❑	❑	❑
10. We were created to live in relationship with God.	❑	❑	❑	❑
11. Moses parted the Red Sea.	❑	❑	❑	❑
12. All good people will go to heaven.	❑	❑	❑	❑
13. The world will end just as described in Revelation.	❑	❑	❑	❑

Discussion Questions

● Which beliefs do you and your partner agree are essential?

● On which beliefs do you disagree regarding what's essential?

● In your opinion, why are the essential statements vital to the Christian faith?

● In your opinion, why are the other statements not essential?

Permission to photocopy this handout from Group's Apply-It-To-Life™ Adult Bible Curriculum granted for local church use.
Copyright © Group Publishing, Inc., Box 481, Loveland, CO 80539.

Know What You Believe

The Point: ▶ We can share our faith with confidence when we know what we believe.

Scripture Focus: 1 Corinthians 15:1-11

Reflecting on God's Word

Each day this week, read one of the following Scripture passages and examine what it says about your faith. Then reflect on how well you are applying the passage's message in your life. List your discoveries in the space under each passage.

Day 1: Hebrews 10:19-25. Jesus Christ gives us confidence before God.

Day 2: James 2:14-26. Only our good deeds can prove our claim to have faith.

Day 3: John 11:25-26. People who trust Jesus will never die spiritually.

Day 4: Romans 3:20-26. God accepts us because of what Jesus did, not what we do.

Day 5: Galatians 1:6-10. Paul condemns anyone who tries to pervert the gospel.

Day 6: John 3:16-21. God sent Jesus to earth to bring us the gift of eternal life.

Beyond Reflection

1. Begin writing your own statement of faith. After listing everything you believe, distinguish between those things you think every Christian should believe and those things that aren't as critical. As much as possible, list scriptural support for all your beliefs. Periodically review your statement of faith and record new insights. You might want to discuss your faith journal with a friend.

2. If you've never read through the entire Bible, plan to do so during the coming months. Many study Bibles have plans for reading through the Bible. To make your experience more meaningful, periodically meet with two or three other adults to discuss your findings.

Next Week's Bible Passages: Acts 8:26-39 and 17:22-34

Permission to photocopy this handout from Group's Apply-It-To-Life™ Adult Bible Curriculum granted for local church use.
Copyright © Group Publishing, Inc., Box 481, Loveland, CO 80539.

Truth in Plain Language

It's important to speak in plain language when we tell others about Christ.

OBJECTIVES

Participants will
- discover the importance of speaking plainly about their faith,
- practice telling someone what it means to be a Christian, and
- explore how Paul and Philip taught others about Christ.

BIBLE BASIS

Look up the Scriptures for this lesson. Then read the following background paragraphs to see how the passages relate to people today.

In **Acts 8:26-39,** the Holy Spirit leads Philip to tell an Ethiopian about Jesus.

ACTS 8:26-39

There is some disagreement about the extent of the land called Ethiopia in the Bible, but it is generally thought to have been south of Egypt along the Nile River. Although it was not as far south as modern Ethiopia, it was still several weeks' journey from Jerusalem.

The Ethiopian in this passage is called a eunuch, which may indicate that he had been emasculated. In the ancient world, it was fairly common for men who served the queen to be emasculated, but the Greek word also refers to other government officials. At the very least, he was a powerful Ethiopian official and apparently a follower of the Jewish religion, for he was returning to Ethiopia after having worshiped at Jerusalem.

Acts 8:26-39 is significant for several reasons. First, Philip followed the Holy Spirit's direction without hesitation. The Holy Spirit knew when the Ethiopian would be ready to hear and accept the message about Jesus. The Holy Spirit knew what the Ethiopian needed and prompted Philip to fulfill that need. Philip's example of obedience can be a model to all Christians.

Second, Philip inquired about the Ethiopian's understanding of Scripture and began from that point in his teaching. All too often, we assume everyone else knows what we know. Consequently, we fail to communicate God's love effectively because we ignore the other person's level of understanding.

Finally, Philip simply explained the good news about Jesus. He didn't grill the Ethiopian about his beliefs or lifestyle. Philip led the man from a point of confusion or misunderstanding to a place of comprehension and faith. As Christians, our goal should be to do the same—to help people understand the message of Christ so they, too, can choose to follow God.

ACTS 17:22-34

In **Acts 17:22-34,** Paul clearly and effectively teaches the people of Athens about Jesus.

Imagine you're sitting alone and a stranger begins to talk to you. The stranger introduces himself and says, "If you only flarfen with your whole heart, you'll become a stargle smippet and be saved from perpetual quigglesnurf."

Would you be confused? Of course you would. Unfortunately, that's how many people feel when we use Christian jargon to tell them about Christ. If we use words that only people in the church understand, we may not be understood when we try to share about Jesus. Throughout his ministry, the Apostle Paul made sure his words were appropriate to the people he was talking to.

In this passage, Paul directed his message to non-Jews rather than his more usual Jewish audience. So instead of explaining how Jesus fulfilled Old Testament prophecies—which was his standard approach with the Jews—Paul began his message by referring to a god the Athenians worshiped.

Paul was taken to the meeting of the Areopagus (Acts 17:18-19) because that council was regarded as the city's keeper of religion. The leaders there would debate new religious philosophies and declare whether a religious idea was suitable for the people of Athens.

The Greeks, for all their knowledge and wisdom, were quite fearful when it came to religion. They worshiped many gods and were afraid to offend any other gods they might not know about. So they erected an altar TO AN

UNKNOWN GOD, seeking to cover all their bases and avoid the wrath of any god they might not be aware of.

It's ironic that the Greeks thought an *unknown* god watched over Athens, the center of Greek knowledge and wisdom. Paul knew that the people really needed to discover the *known* God. Paul spoke to the Athenians on their own level, fully aware of their beliefs and clearly explaining God's working in terms they could understand.

Acts 17:32-34 tells us that a few believed Paul and became followers. But not everyone who listened to Paul chose to follow God. Some even sneered. That also happens today. Yet, by telling people about Jesus in plain language, we can open the door to Christ for the people we work with, live with, or meet on the street. Moreover, we can trust the Holy Spirit to guide and help us as we do so.

THIS LESSON AT A GLANCE

Section	Minutes	What Participants Will Do	Supplies
OPENING	*up to 10*	**STRANGE WORLDS**—Tell about times they've felt like foreigners.	
BIBLE EXPLORATION AND APPLICATION	*25 to 35*	☐ *Option 1:* **CONFUSE ME**—Discover how difficult it can be to understand the language of faith and examine Paul's speech in Acts 17:22-31.	Bibles
	15 to 25	☐ *Option 2:* **SIMPLE AND TRUE**—Explore Philip's encounter with the Ethiopian in Acts 8:26-39 and practice telling one another what it means to be a Christian.	Bibles
CLOSING	*10 to 15*	**REAL LIFE**—Brainstorm ways to share their faith in everyday situations.	Bibles, pencils, paper
FOR EXTRA TIME	*up to 5*	**SIMPLE PRAYER**—Write a simple prayer to share with someone who wants to become a Christian.	3x5 cards, pencils
	up to 10	**FAITH-SHARING CONFIDENCE**—Describe times they've told others what it means to be a Christian.	
	up to 10	**DEFINING CHRISTIAN JARGON**—List Christian jargon words or phrases and explore their meanings.	Bibles, paper, pencils

Strange Worlds

(up to 10 minutes)

Begin class with prayer. Encourage class members to get involved in the discussions and activities during the study.

Form trios. Have everyone tell a brief story about a time he or she felt like a stranger or foreigner. Participants might tell about times they were in a foreign country or were among people who spoke a different language or had completely different interests. Encourage people to focus on how they felt and what they learned in those circumstances.

Ask the following questions to help trios discuss these experiences:

● **What did it feel like to be a stranger or foreigner?** (I felt uncomfortable; I felt uneasy; I didn't know how to act.)

● **What was most uncomfortable for you?** (I didn't understand the language; I thought people didn't like me.)

● **How might the way you felt be like the way non-Christians feel when they're among Christians?** (It's probably similar; when we talk about our faith, it probably seems foreign to non-Christians.)

● **How did you bridge the gap and overcome your feelings of being a foreigner?** (I didn't; I learned to communicate; I became more accustomed to their language and customs.)

Say: **We all get uncomfortable in situations in which we don't understand what others are talking about. However, when we talk about our faith we often use confusing or unclear words and phrases that make people outside the church uncomfortable.** ▷ **Today we're going to explore the importance of speaking plainly when we share our faith with others.**

T H E   P O I N T ▷

□ **O P T I O N   1 :**

Confuse Me

(25 to 35 minutes)

Form two teams. Say: **I'm going to give each team an unusual message to share with the other team and a list of rules for sharing that message. After you've been given your instructions, take five minutes to discuss how you'll get the other team to understand your message.**

Call one person from each team aside one at a time and give each representative one of the following instructions. Repeat your instructions for them if necessary.

T E A C H E R
TIP

If you have more than 12 class members, form four or six teams and assign each message to half of the teams. You may need to send teams to different corners of the room or adjoining rooms to allow teams to work on this activity at the same time.

Team 1: You must communicate the following message without using any words (written or spoken). You may use motions and facial expressions, but that's all. Your message is "Three wise elephants know no more than one foolish ape."

Team 2: You must communicate the following message without using any words (written or spoken). You may use motions and nonword sounds, but that's all. Your message is "Fine feathered friends often become fiends when framed."

Give teams five minutes to discuss their strategies for communicating their messages. Then have each team present its message. Afterward, tell teams what the actual messages were and have them give each other a round of applause for their efforts.

Form groups of four that contain members from both teams. Have groups discuss the following questions. Ask:

● **What was it like to try to communicate your message to the other team?** (It was difficult; we weren't sure how to do it; I felt ridiculous.)

● **How is that like how you feel when you tell someone about your faith? How is it different?** (I'm a little unsure about how to tell someone about Christ; each of us has different ideas about sharing our faith.)

● **How did you feel when you were trying to figure out the other team's message?** (Frustrated; confused; I had no idea what the message was.)

● **How might that be like the way people feel when we tell them about Jesus? How might it be different?** (They don't hear what we're saying; the words sound like gibberish; we can use a normal means of communication.)

● **What are some Christian words or phrases we use that non-Christians might not understand?** (Salvation; saved; born-again; sanctification; reconciliation.)

● **How does the use of this Christian jargon affect non-Christians?** (They don't understand what it means; they feel uncomfortable with those words; they feel inferior because they don't know what the words mean.)

Have groups share their insights with the whole class. Then have group members read **Acts 17:22-31** and discuss the following questions.

● **What did Paul refer to first as he began speaking to the leaders of Athens?** (Things they knew about; familiar idols; he complimented them for being religious.)

● **What kind of language did Paul use in talking with them?** (General language; language they would relate to.)

● **What comforting thoughts did he give?** (That God isn't far from us; that we are God's offspring.)

BIBLE INSIGHT

In Acts 17:28, Paul appeals to the interest and knowledge of the Athenians by quoting two poets whose sayings the Athenians would be familiar with. The first, "In him we live and move and have our being," is from Epimenides (about 600 B.C.). The second, "We are his offspring," is from Aratus (around 250 B.C.). By quoting these poets, Paul probably gained respect from the intellectuals he was talking with. In so doing, he also made them look more favorably on the message he was presenting.

● **Who did Paul quote?** (Someone they knew; the Athenians' own poets.)

● **What are the differences between the way you communicated your message to the other team and the way Paul communicated his message?** (Paul communicated through clear language; Paul related his message to what the people knew; Paul knew what he was doing.)

● **How can we use Paul's approach in telling others about our faith?** (We should relate to people on their own level; we should use language people understand; we should compliment people instead of condemn them.)

Have groups share their insights with the rest of the class. Then say: **In this activity, the messages we tried to communicate were meaningless. But Paul's message—the message of what God has done for us—is the most important message we can possibly share with others.**

When we talk about our faith, we sometimes use confusing language. When we do, people have a hard time understanding what we're saying. ▷ **That's why it's important to speak in words people will understand when we tell them about our faith.**

THE POINT ▷

■■■■■■■■■■■■■■■■■■■■■■■■■■■■

FOR *Even Deeper* **DISCUSSION**

Form groups of four or fewer and discuss the following questions:

● Sometimes Jesus purposely made his message hard to understand (see Matthew 13:10-17). Why do you think he did that? Should we ever follow that example today? Explain.

● Paul began his message about Jesus by referring to the Athenians' gods. What "gods" do people worship today? Explain. How do people's gods keep them from understanding God's message? How could we use those gods to lead into a conversation about the true God?

■■■■■■■■■■■■■■■■■■■■■■■■■■■■

☐ **OPTION 2:**

Simple and True

(15 to 25 minutes)

Say: **Philip, a leader in the Jerusalem church, had an opportunity to tell someone from another culture about Jesus. Let's take a look at how that went.**

Form pairs. Have pairs read **Acts 8:26-39.** Then have partners discuss the following questions and, after discussing all three, report their answers to the rest of the class.

● **How did Philip approach the Ethiopian?** (He listened first; he followed what God told him to do; he asked if the Ethiopian understood Isaiah.)

● **What did Philip use to tell the Ethiopian about Jesus?** (The words he was reading from Isaiah; passages of Scripture.)

● **Because the Ethiopian ended up believing in Jesus, what can we assume about the language Philip used?** (It was clear; it made sense to the Ethiopian.)

After five minutes, have volunteers share their discoveries from the Scriptures. Then say: **Stay with your partner and briefly tell each other what being a Christian means to you. Avoid using "Christian" words; simply**  **speak in plain language and from your own faith experience. You have five minutes.**

After five minutes, ask:

● **What's the most difficult thing to communicate when we're telling someone about Christ?** (What being a Christian really feels like; how much God loves us; that we don't know everything.)

● **What can Philip's example teach us about telling others about Christ?** (We need to listen to the Holy Spirit; we should speak in clear language; our goal is to help others understand the Scriptures.)

Encourage partners to express appreciation to each other for discussing what being a Christian means to them. Remind people to sincerely thank each other for opening up and sharing in this activity.

TEACHER TIP

If you didn't complete Option 1, you might want half of your pairs to look up Acts 17:22-31 and relate the discussion questions to Paul and the Athenians instead of Philip and the Ethiopian. Then have people with different passages share their insights with each other.

◀ **THE POINT**

■■■■■■■■■■■■■■■■■■■■■■■■■■■

FOR *Even Deeper* DISCUSSION

Form groups of four or fewer and discuss the following questions:

● Think of a cultural group that speaks your language but is very different from yours. What would it be like to share your faith with someone from that group? How would you have to modify what you say to communicate your message to that person?

● How would you share your faith with someone who couldn't speak your language?

● St. Francis of Assisi said, "Preach the gospel all the time. If necessary, use words." What did he mean by that? Would it be possible to explain, without using words, what God did through Jesus? Explain.

■■■■■■■■■■■■■■■■■■■■■■■■■■■

The "Apply-It-To-Life This Week" handout (p. 38) helps people further explore the issues uncovered in today's class. Give everyone a photocopy of the handout. Encourage class members to take time during the coming week to explore the questions and activities listed on the handout.

CLOSING

Real Life

(10 to 15 minutes)

If you completed Option 1, have people remain in their foursomes. If you completed Option 2, have each pair join another pair to form a foursome.

Give each group a sheet of paper and a pencil. Say: **In your group, brainstorm the places and times you wish you could speak up about your faith. Think of real-life situations you experience. For example, if you wish you could talk about your faith with your boss, list that situation on your paper. Be specific about the situations.**

After about five minutes, call time. Say: **Now, starting with the first situation on your list, use what you've**

THE POINT ▷

already learned about ▷ speaking in plain language when you talk about your faith. Discuss practical ways to tell that person or those people about Christ. You may want to refer to Acts 8:26-39; 17:22-34; or any other verses for ideas on how to share your faith naturally. In five minutes, I'll ask you to share your ideas.

After about five minutes, have volunteers report ideas for sharing their faith in specific situations. Solicit new ideas from the rest of the class for each situation.

Say: **We don't need to pound people over the head with Christian jargon to help them understand what God has done for them through Jesus. When we talk about our own faith, people can catch a glimpse of our passion and love for Christ. Moreover, when we speak in terms others understand, people can learn what it means to be a Christian.**

Close the session by having people pray in their groups for God to give them the right words when they tell others about Christ.

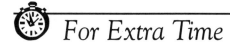

For Extra Time

SIMPLE PRAYER
(up to 5 minutes)

Form groups of four. Give each person a 3×5 card and a pencil. Say: **On your 3×5 card, compose a simple prayer you can share with a non-Christian who wants to become a Christian. Keep your card with you as a reminder to reach out to others by speaking plainly about your own faith experience.**

FAITH-SHARING CONFIDENCE
(up to 10 minutes)

To build participants' confidence, have volunteers tell class members about times they've told others about Jesus or what it means to be a Christian. Have people briefly explain how they felt in the situation and what, if anything, resulted.

Then have people form groups of four or fewer to close in prayer. Before groups pray, have class members share concerns or names of people they'd like the group to pray for. Remind people to ask God to help them speak in plain language when they tell others about Christ.

DEFINING CHRISTIAN JARGON
(up to 10 minutes)

Have people brainstorm a list of Christian jargon (words or phrases that have specifically Christian meanings). Then have groups of four or fewer examine and define one or more of the words and share their findings with the whole class.

Truth in Plain Language

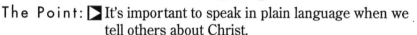

The Point: ▶ It's important to speak in plain language when we tell others about Christ.

Scripture Focus: Acts 8:26-39 and 17:22-34

Reflecting on God's Word

Each day this week, read one of the following Scriptures. Learn how the people in the passages lived out or shared their faith. Think of how you might apply these ideas to your own everyday evangelism. List your discoveries in the space under each passage.

Day 1: Acts 3:11-26. Peter tells Jews about Jesus.

Day 2: Acts 4:1-22. Peter and John refuse to stop speaking about Jesus.

Day 3: Acts 9:26-31. Paul preaches fearlessly about Jesus.

Day 4: Acts 10:1-48. Peter tells Cornelius about Jesus.

Day 5: Acts 14:8-18. Paul and Barnabas refuse to be treated like gods.

Day 6: Acts 17:1-4. Paul and Silas explain that Jesus is the Messiah.

"Successful witnessing is simply taking the initiative to share Christ in the power of the Holy Spirit—and leaving the results to God."—Bill Bright, *Witnessing Without Fear* (Thomas Nelson Publishers)

Beyond Reflection

1. Read the Bill Bright statement in the box above and think about the following questions:
- Do you agree or disagree with the statement? Why?
- How do we know when and how to take the initiative?
- How will you take the initiative to share Christ this week?

2. Read chapter 24 of Charles Colson's *The Body* (Word Publishing) and discuss it with a group of friends. This chapter, titled "Being His Witnesses," explores the role of evangelism in the church.

3. Choose one person you'd like to share your faith with. Start praying that God will provide the opportunity to do so. Work on developing your relationship with that person. Think through what you might say and be ready to say it when the opportunity arises. As you pray for and speak with this person, seek the Holy Spirit's guidance.

Next Week's Bible Passages: Philippians 2:1-5; Titus 2:7-8; and James 2:14-26

Permission to photocopy this handout from Group's Apply-It-To-Life™ Adult Bible Curriculum granted for local church use.
Copyright © Group Publishing, Inc., Box 481, Loveland, CO 80539.

Actions Speak Louder

Our actions can be a powerful witness for Christ.

◀ THE POINT

OBJECTIVES

Participants will
- discuss how love is communicated through actions,
- examine what the Bible teaches about the necessity of doing good to others, and
- list specific ways they can share their faith through their actions.

BIBLE BASIS

Look up the Scriptures for this lesson. Then read the following background paragraphs to see how the passages relate to people today.

James 2:14-26 teaches that true faith is demonstrated through good deeds.

JAMES 2:14-26

Christians trying to be positive witnesses for Christ often make one of two errors. Some act as though all they need to do is live a good life among non-Christians, while others rely almost entirely on their words to lead others to Christ. The Bible warns us to avoid both extremes. James addresses the latter in James 2:14-26.

The passage presents several difficulties, the most significant being the seeming contradiction between Paul's teaching that we are justified by faith apart from works (Romans 3:28) and James' assertion that we are justified by what we do and not by faith alone (James 2:24).

However, the contradiction is more apparent than real. In Romans 3, Paul explains how a person becomes a Christian. In James 2, James discusses how someone can validate a claim to have faith. Romans 3 teaches that we are made righteous before God strictly on the basis of faith; James 2:14-26 demonstrates that valid claims of having faith will be accompanied by good works.

James restates his thesis several times (James 2:14, 20, 24, and 26), and, although he words it differently each time, the gist remains the same: Claims to have faith mean nothing. The only thing that matters is authentic faith that always shows itself in good deeds.

James can make this bold assertion for several reasons. First, kind words are nice, but they're useless when not followed by kind actions (verses 15-17). In addition, authentic faith and good deeds are so inseparable that people who claim to believe but don't evidence it through good deeds are as convincing as the demons who do likewise (verses 18-19). Finally, the stories of Abraham (verses 21-24) and Rahab (verses 25-26) offer compelling biblical evidence that living faith always reveals itself in righteous actions. In sum, faith without works is no more a living faith than a corpse without breath is a living person.

PHILIPPIANS 2:1-5

In **Philippians 2:1-5,** Paul encourages us to imitate Christ's example of serving others.

Although the Christians at Philippi were being persecuted, they still needed to witness to their persecutors through their actions. In fact, the Philippians were to live in a manner worthy of the gospel whatever their circumstances might be (see Philippians 1:27-30).

Paul describes one element of a life worthy of the gospel in Philippians 2:1-5. He wanted the Philippians to have the same mind, love, and purpose. More specifically, they were to adopt the sacrificial attitude Christ demonstrated when he left the glory of heaven and came to earth as a humble servant (Philippians 2:6-11). If the Philippians imitated Christ in this manner, they'd look out for each other's interests and, in so doing, present a powerful image of the gospel for everyone to see.

TITUS 2:7-8

In **Titus 2:7-8,** Paul instructs Titus to live in such a way that no one can criticize him.

It was not uncommon for non-Christians to regard the early church as a threat to society. Consequently, church leaders such as Paul took special care to avoid any unnecessary conflicts with the social mores of the day. To that end, Paul instructed Titus to teach his church members to live in such a way that people outside the church could make no valid accusation against them.

On the one hand, different groups within the church needed to conform to society's expectations of good citizens (Titus 2:1-6). However, everyone was to perform good deeds. Also, if Titus' church members followed his example of living *and* speaking responsibly, non-Christians wouldn't have anything for which they could validly criticize them.

God calls us to reach out to others with the message of Christ's love. But *telling* people about God's love is just part of the job. Following Jesus' example of actually loving others is often the best way to convince people that God loves them. Use this lesson to help your class members learn how to share their faith with non-Christians through all they do.

THIS LESSON AT A GLANCE

Section	Minutes	What Participants Will Do	Supplies
OPENING	up to 10	**WHEN SOMEONE CARED**—Tell of times they felt loved.	
BIBLE EXPLORATION AND APPLICATION	25 to 35	☐ Option 1: **AUTHENTIC FAITH**—Show each other they care, discover the teaching of James 2:14-26, and list some ways to use their actions to demonstrate their faith in Christ.	Bibles, "Proving Our Faith" handouts (p. 48), pencils, coffee supplies, tea bags, hot water, cups, pastries, fruit, napkins
	15 to 25	☐ Option 2: **IMAGES OF CHRIST**—Try to copy a drawing of Jesus, then study Philippians 2:1-5; Titus 2:7-8; and James 2:14-17 to learn how to present accurate images of Christ through their actions.	Bibles, drawing of Jesus washing the disciples' feet (p. 49) paper, pencils
CLOSING	up to 10	**ONE ACTION**—Choose a way to show Christ's love in the coming week and commit to it.	Bibles
FOR EXTRA TIME	up to 10	**FAITH IN ACTION**—Brainstorm and plan one way to reach out to non-Christians in the community.	
	up to 10	**JAMES AND PAUL**—Compare and contrast what James and Paul teach about justification.	Bibles, Bible commentaries, Bible encyclopedia

When Someone Cared

(up to 10 minutes)

To begin the class, form groups of four or fewer. Have everyone take turns completing the following sentence: "One time I felt truly loved was…"

After everyone has told about a time he or she felt loved, have group members discuss the following questions. Then gather people together and have volunteers share insights from their discussions. Ask:

● **What caused you to feel loved in the situation you described?** (Someone took an interest in me; someone helped me out when I was in need.)

● **What part did someone's words play in your situation?** (My friend talked to me when I was down; my friend shared encouraging words.)

● **What part did someone's actions play in your situation?** (My friend cooked dinner for me; a friend gave me a hug when I needed it.)

Say: **Last week we learned that we need to use plain language when we're telling others about Jesus. However, if our actions don't support our words, people won't listen to us for long no matter how clearly we speak. Today we're going to explore how** ▷ **our actions can be a powerful witness for Christ.**

 **THE POINT** ▷

□ OPTION 1:

Authentic Faith

(25 to 35 minutes)

Before class, make one photocopy of the "Proving Our Faith" handout (p. 48) for each person.

On a table, arrange pastries, fruit, napkins, and the materials necessary for making instant coffee and hot tea.

Say: **Because this lesson is about showing our faith through our deeds, take the next five minutes to let your actions do the talking to the people around you. Without saying a word, show your Christian love to the rest of the class.**

Say nothing more and watch how people react. If they don't know what to do, set an example by serving coffee and a doughnut to someone or by giving someone a hug or a shoulder rub.

After five minutes, get everyone's attention and have people re-form their groups from the Opening activity. Encourage anyone who hasn't already gotten something to eat or drink to do so now. Then direct group members to discuss the following questions. After each question, ask volunteers to report their groups' responses to the rest of the class. Ask:

● **What was your reaction to being asked to show your Christian love? to being shown Christian love?** (I wanted to show love to my friend; I wasn't quite sure what I should do; I wanted someone to do something for me first; I wished Christians were like this more often.)

● **What was your reaction to not being allowed to speak while you were showing Christian love?** (It made it hard to communicate my exact feelings; my actions seemed more meaningful; I focused more on the way I acted toward others.)

● **How is the way we just acted similar to the way Christians act among non-Christians? How is it different?** (We're usually kind to people; we focus more on telling people about God's love than on showing it; sometimes our words and our actions aren't consistent.)

Say: **It's important to be ready to tell others about our faith in Christ, but that isn't enough. We also need to support our claim to be Christians by the things we do. Let's examine James 2:14-26 to see how and why we're to do this.**

Give each person a copy of the "Proving Our Faith" handout and a pencil. Have group members read the instructions at the top of the handout and then complete it together.

Allow groups at least 10 minutes to work through the handout, then get everyone's attention. Ask groups to summarize their conclusions about **James 2:14-26** for the rest of the class. Encourage people to ask any questions they still have about the Scripture passage. Then instruct groups to discuss the following questions, reporting their answers to the rest of the class after each question. Ask:

● **Why are non-Christians sometimes unreceptive to the gospel?** (They think Christians are hypocrites; they don't understand us when we attempt to explain the gospel; they've been hurt by Christians in the past.)

● **How do our actions affect non-Christians' opinions of us?** (When we're loving, non-Christians have a high opinion of us; non-Christians won't listen to what we say if our actions don't support our words.)

● **How does acting on our faith draw others to Christ?** (People see the way we act and want to know why; people are intrigued by someone who loves them unconditionally; non-

The Greek word *dikaioō* means "to justify, vindicate, or treat as just" (see Romans 3:24, 26, 28, 30 and James 2:21, 24, 25). Paul uses the word in Romans 3 with reference to being made right before God. James uses it in James 2 within the context of substantiating one's claim to have faith. James argues that the only faith that justifies a person is the faith that shows itself through what it does.

Christians form a favorable opinion of God when we represent him accurately.)

● **In what specific ways can you substantiate your claim to have faith?** (I can feed the hungry and provide shelter for the homeless; I can spend time with a friend who's lost a spouse; I can watch my neighbor's kids; I can forgive someone who's spread rumors about me.)

Say: **Because our actions can be a powerful witness for Christ, we need to think carefully about how to give people an accurate impression of Christ and his love for them. Take several minutes to fill out the "Bible Application" section of your handout. You probably won't have time right now to complete it, but this will get you started thinking in the right direction.**

After several minutes, say: **The most effective way to draw non-Christians to Christ is to show them and tell them about God's love for them in Jesus Christ. Take the handout home, work on it during the coming weeks, and refer to it periodically. It will help you evaluate your progress and remind you that ▷our actions can be a powerful witness for Christ.**

T H E   P O I N T ▷

T H E   P O I N T ▷

TEACHER

TIP

To help people remember specific ways to show their faith, hang a sheet of newsprint where everyone can see it and write class members' suggestions on it.

■■■■■■■■■■■■■■■■■■■■■■■■■■■■■

**FOR *Even Deeper*
DISCUSSION**

Form groups of four or fewer and discuss the following questions:

● Is there any contradiction between Paul's teaching that we're justified by faith apart from works (Romans 3:28) and James' that we're justified by what we do and not by faith alone (James 2:24)? Explain.

● To what extent do people "prove" they're Christians by doing good? Is everyone who does good a Christian? Are there any other ways to tell if someone is or is not a Christian?

■■■■■■■■■■■■■■■■■■■■■■■■■■■■

□ **OPTION 2:**

Images of Christ

(15 to 25 minutes)

Form trios. Give each person a sheet of paper and a pencil. Tell people you're going to show them a picture you want them to reproduce as well as they can. Then show each trio the drawing on page 49 of Jesus washing the disciples' feet. However, don't allow anyone to see the picture for longer than 5 seconds.

After two minutes, have trio members compare their

drawings. Then instruct trio members to discuss the following questions. Ask volunteers to report their trios' responses after each question. Ask:

● **What was the picture I showed you?** The picture is of Jesus washing the disciples' feet. Some people may have different ideas of what the picture is. If so, discuss the impossibility of reproducing a picture when we're mistaken about what it is.

● **Was it easy or difficult for you to draw the picture? Explain.** (It was difficult because I didn't get a good look at the picture; it was easy to draw the general outline, but I missed a lot of details.)

● **How well would people looking at your picture know what the original looked like?** (Their view of the original would be completely inaccurate; most people would recognize the important parts; they'd have as many wrong ideas as right ones.)

Say: **Every day we draw pictures of Christ with our lives. In many cases, these pictures are the only images of Christ that non-Christians around us have, so we need to make sure we're representing Christ accurately. The Bible tells us what our images of Christ should look like.**

Have trio members number off from one to three. Send the ones to one area of the room, the twos to another, and so on. Assign the ones **Titus 2:7-8,** the twos **Philippians 2:1-5,** and the threes **James 2:14-17.** Tell groups to read their assigned passages then list what they teach about how Christians should represent Christ.

After five minutes, instruct people to return to their original trios and tell each other what they've learned. Then direct trios to discuss the following questions. Ask volunteers to summarize their trios' answers after each question. Ask:

● **What images of Christ do Christians present to non-Christians?** (Christ loves everyone equally; Christ doesn't care about people's physical needs; Christ is a hypocrite; Christ always wants what's best for us.)

● **What images of Christ should we present?** (Christ cares about every human need; Christ wants people to live fulfilled lives; Christ loves everyone unconditionally.)

● **In what specific ways can you present a truer picture of Christ through your actions?** (I can give food or shelter to people who need it; I can befriend someone who's lonely; I can help a co-worker struggling to keep up; I can give our time to a community service project.)

● **What positive results will presenting accurate images of Christ produce?** (When people feel God's love from someone, they want to know more about that

TEACHER **TIP**

If you have more than 21 class members, divide the numbered groups into smaller groups of four or fewer.

BIBLE INSIGHT

Suspicion of Christianity arose for a number of reasons. For example, some non-Christians interpreted the language of the Lord's Supper ("eating the body and drinking the blood") literally and thus charged Christians with cannibalism. Also, the Christian emphasis on "love," "love feasts," and being "brothers and sisters" (terms for husbands and wives in some circles) provoked some non-Christians to accuse Christians of engaging in incestuous orgies. Finally, non-Christians neither understood nor accepted the Christian refusal to worship the state gods.

love; our examples give other people a positive example to follow; people will form favorable opinions of God.)

THE POINT ▷

Say: **Because actions almost always say a lot more than words,** ▷ **our actions can be a powerful witness for Christ. That's why it's important to act in a way that honors God and makes others want a relationship with him. One way we present an accurate image of Christ is by showing each other the kind of love Christ shows us. Practice showing love by completing the following sentence to the other members of your trio: "I see Christ in you when . . ."**

Provide an example by affirming one or two members of the class. For instance, you might say, "I see Christ in you when you speak the truth boldly" or "I see Christ when you greet everyone in class warmly."

■■■■■■■■■■■■■■■■■■■■■■■■■■■■■■

FOR *Even Deeper* **DISCUSSION**

Form groups of four or fewer and discuss the following questions:

● Several times Paul instructed Christians to conform to the social standards of that time so non-Christians would think well of them (Ephesians 5:22–6:9; Colossians 3:18–4:1; and Titus 2:1-8). To what extent should we adapt ourselves to society? How can we know when to conform and when to dissent?

● In Philippians 2:2, Paul commands the Christians at Philippi to be "like-minded." Does this mean Christians are to think the same way? Explain. How can the church balance unity and diversity? What can non-Christians learn about Christ from this?

■■■■■■■■■■■■■■■■■■■■■■■■■■■■■■

APPLY▪IT▪TO **LIFE** **THIS WEEK**

The "Apply-It-To-Life This Week" handout (p. 50) helps people further explore the issues uncovered in today's class. Give everyone a photocopy of the handout. Encourage class members to take time during the coming week to explore the questions and activities listed on the handout.

One Action

(up to 10 minutes)

Have people remain in their groups from the previous activity. Instruct groups to read **Ephesians 5:1-2.** Then have group members each name specific ways they can be witnesses for Christ through their actions. Encourage people to be specific about what they'll do. For example, someone might deliver cookies or a meal to a person who's recently been through a tough time. Someone else might offer to baby-sit so the parent(s) can have a free night. Ask group members to make verbal commitments to each other to act on their ideas during the coming week.

After five minutes, get everyone's attention. Say: **Today's lesson reminds us that being a living witness for Christ is just as important as telling others what we believe. Let's commit together to witness for Christ through our words and our actions.**   ◀ THE POINT

For Extra Time

FAITH IN ACTION

(up to 10 minutes)

Have class members brainstorm ways they can reach out as a group in Christian love to non-Christians in the community. For example, they might plan a barbecue for people in the church neighborhood or paint or repair someone's home. Encourage the class to select the best idea and to begin planning the outreach activity.

JAMES AND PAUL

(up to 10 minutes)

Form groups of four. Direct group members to compare and contrast Paul's teaching concerning "justification" in Romans 3:27-31 with James' teaching in James 2:14-26. If possible, provide Bible commentaries and a Bible encyclopedia to help people explore the passages and their contexts.

▪ PROVING OUR FAITH

Read James 2:14-26, then discuss the questions below with your group members. Record any insights in the space provided. You have approximately 10 minutes to complete the "Bible Exploration" portion of the handout.

1 How does James describe claims of faith that aren't accompanied by good works?

2 What does this imply about the relationship between faith and works? about the nature of faith?

3 Read the FYI box at the bottom of the handout. In what way are people "justified" by works (James 2:24)?

4 What primary question do you think this passage was written to answer:

- What is the nature of true faith?

- What is the relationship between faith and works?

- How is true faith demonstrated?

- How does one validate one's claim to have faith?

- Some other question.

5 What answer does the passage give to this question?

BIBLE APPLICATION

In the left column, write the names of non-Christian friends, relatives, neighbors, or co-workers who know you're a Christian. Then, in the right column, write one specific way you can validate your claim to faith by showing that person God's love.

The Greek word *dikaioō* means "to justify, vindicate, or treat as just" (see Romans 3:24, 26, 28, 30 and James 2:21, 24, 25). Paul uses the word in Romans 3 with reference to being made right with God. However, *dikaioō* can also refer to being declared innocent by a court or to being regarded as right by people.

Permission to photocopy this handout from Group's Apply-It-To-Life™ Adult Bible Curriculum granted for local church use.
Copyright © Group Publishing, Inc., Box 481, Loveland, CO 80539.

Actions Speak Louder

The Point: ▶ Our actions can be a powerful witness for Christ.
Scripture Focus: James 2:14-26; Philippians 2:1-5; and Titus 2:7-8

Reflecting on God's Word

Each day this week, read one of the following Scriptures and examine what it says about acting in love toward non-Christians. Then examine how well you are applying the message of the passage in your life. List your discoveries in the space under each passage.

Day 1: Luke 6:27-36. Jesus wants us to love people even when they don't love us in return.

Day 2: Leviticus 19:33-34. We shouldn't take advantage of people who are weaker than we.

Day 3: Ephesians 5:1-2. We imitate God by loving others as Christ loved us.

Day 4: 1 Peter 2:13-17. We honor God by living peaceably with all people.

Day 5: Isaiah 1:11-17. God values righteous lives more than religious deeds.

Day 6: Luke 10:25-37. We love our neighbors by meeting their needs.

Beyond Reflection

1. Look for opportunities to put your faith into action in your community. For example, you might volunteer at a shelter for the homeless, help a neighbor haul topsoil, or visit people in a nursing home or a detention center. As you put your faith into action, remember to focus on serving others without expecting anything in return.

2. Ask your closest friends to rate how well you exemplify Christ in your life. Be prepared for less-than-perfect ratings. Ask your friends to honestly tell you ways you could improve. Then pray together for wisdom to be more Christlike. Read Ephesians 4:17-32 as a discussion starter about what a life of faith should be like. Then put the ideas you discover into practice.

Next Week's Bible Passages: Matthew 28:18-20; 2 Timothy 1:5-11; and 1 Peter 4:7-11

Permission to photocopy this handout from Group's Apply-It-To-Life™ Adult Bible Curriculum granted for local church use.
Copyright © Group Publishing, Inc., Box 481, Loveland, CO 80539.

Gifted to Tell

We can use our unique gifts and abilities to teach others about Jesus.

OBJECTIVES

Participants will
- explore their gifts and abilities,
- determine how they can follow Christ's command to share the gospel, and
- learn what kind of everyday evangelist they're most like.

BIBLE BASIS

Look up the Scriptures for this lesson. Then read the following background paragraphs to see how the passages relate to people today.

In **Matthew 28:18-20,** Jesus commands his disciples to teach every nation about him.

MATTHEW 28:18-20

This familiar passage is often called the Great Commission, but it's more than just a commission or command. It's a powerful encouragement to Jesus' first disciples and to us, their successors, to spread the good news about Jesus Christ throughout the world.

Earlier Jesus had sent the 12 disciples out to preach and to heal. However, that mission had been restricted specifically to the "lost sheep" of Israel (Matthew 10:5-8). But after his resurrection from the dead, Jesus expanded the disciples' mission field. He sent them to the entire world.

The Great Commission gives a powerful admonition to spread God's message around the world. Sending missionaries to foreign countries is part of that commission, but there's also a message for every Christian. God has given each of us special gifts and abilities, and we can use them to let our own "world" know about the God we serve. God wants us to be everyday evangelists who tell the people around us about him through our actions and words. The Holy Spirit goes with us at all times to help us do that.

2 TIMOTHY 1:5-11

In **2 Timothy 1:5-11,** Paul encourages Timothy to be bold in telling others about Jesus.

Timothy had probably come to faith in Jesus through Paul's ministry (1 Timothy 1:2). At the very least, Paul had helped Timothy grow as a Christian, so it was natural for Paul to regard Timothy in some way as his own son (2 Timothy 1:2).

In 2 Timothy 1:5-11, Paul's admonitions give the impression that Timothy wasn't offering the strong, clear leadership the church at Ephesus needed. So Paul gently but firmly encouraged Timothy to put his timidity behind him and to depend on the Holy Spirit for the boldness to tell others about Jesus. As Timothy allowed the Spirit to control his life, he would see God's power, love, and self-discipline coming out in all he did.

To lend strength to his encouragement toward boldness, Paul reminded Timothy why he should be bold in telling others about Jesus. Paul pointed out what God had done for him through Jesus. He reminded Timothy that gratitude and obedience to God should permeate all we do.

Paul's encouragement of Timothy applies to us as well. Fear of rejection or even suffering should never deter us from telling others about the One who's done so much for us and who can do the same for them.

1 PETER 4:7-11

1 Peter 4:7-11 describes the diversity of gifts within the body of believers.

Peter begins this passage by giving an overarching principle for the use of our gifts—above all else, we're to love each other. He says—much as Paul does in 1 Corinthians 13—that love is to govern the use of spiritual gifts. We're to lovingly use our gifts to build others up and to draw people to Christ.

Peter also suggests that each person's gifts and abilities are vital to the body of Christ. In addition, Peter reminds us we're to *use* the gifts we've been given by God's grace and not let them stagnate. But perhaps most important, Peter gives a specific reason for our using these gifts to serve God: so God may be praised in all we do. In sum, we should use them to help other Christians grow in their relationships with God and to draw non-Christians toward a relationship with God through Jesus.

In 1 Peter 4:11, Peter implies that living a good Christian life is seldom enough. We also need to share our faith through our words. He encourages us to use the Scriptures as we let others know what God has done for us.

When we consider the diversity of talents and abilities we've been given and Jesus' command in the Great Commission, we can begin to see how each of us might have a different role in drawing others toward Jesus. No two people are the same; God has given each of us different gifts and personalities. God wants to use each one of us in a special way to spread his message to others. This lesson will help people discover how they can use their individual gifts and abilities to share the good news of Jesus Christ.

THIS LESSON AT A GLANCE

Section	Minutes	What Participants Will Do	Supplies
OPENING	*up to 10*	**UNSURE**—Explore their fears of telling others about Christ.	Chalkboard and chalk, or newsprint and marker
BIBLE EXPLORATION AND APPLICATION	*15 to 25*	☐ *Option 1:* **EVERY WHICH WAY**—Discover how each person has a unique perspective, read Matthew 28:18-20, and examine how our gifts and abilities can help us tell others about Jesus.	Bibles, "What Do You See?" handouts (p. 60), pencils
	25 to 35	☐ *Option 2:* **FINDING YOUR COMFORT ZONE**—Evaluate statements pertaining to various abilities and explore how Timothy 1:5-11 and 1 Peter 4:7-11 relate to everyday evangelism.	Bibles, paper, marker, tape, "Everyday Evangelists" handouts (p. 61), pencils
CLOSING	*up to 10*	**GOD BE WITH US**—Determine how they'll support one another's evangelistic efforts and pray for God's strength as they reach out to non-Christians.	Paper, pencils
FOR EXTRA TIME	*up to 5*	**COURSE REFLECTION**—Think about how this course has affected their lives.	
	up to 10	**FOLLOW ME**—Examine Jesus' calling of his disciples and discuss how our methods should be the same as (or different from) his.	Bibles

Unsure

(up to 10 minutes)

THE POINT ▷

As you begin class, say: **Today, in our last class on evangelism for every day, we're going to see how ▷ we can use our unique gifts and abilities to teach others about Christ.**

Open with prayer. Encourage class members to get involved in the discussions and activities during the study.

Form pairs. Have partners take turns completing the following sentence: "The thing that scares me most about sharing my faith is ..."

Give people a few moments to discuss their fears, then have them call out their fears so you can list them on a chalkboard or a sheet of newsprint. Then have each pair join another pair to create a foursome. Instruct people to refer to the list you've just made and to answer the following questions in their foursomes. Ask:

● **Based on this list, what conclusions can you draw about our fears?** (We have many different fears; we all have similar concerns.)

● **How might we overcome these fears so we can better tell others about Christ?** (Form support groups; trust God; work as a team.)

● **How does this list of fears reflect the diversity of gifts and abilities in our class?** (Some people are afraid of rejection; some of us are better equipped to share our faith than others; some people don't have many fears.)

Say: **Our fears often reflect a lack of confidence in our ability to speak in public or to communicate clearly. But as we said at the beginning of this course, you don't have to be a great public speaker to be an everyday evangelist. Today we're going to explore how ▷ we can use our unique gifts and abilities to tell other people about Jesus.**

THE POINT ▷

□ **OPTION 1:**

Every Which Way

(15 to 25 minutes)

Before class, make one photocopy of the "What Do You See?" handout (p. 60) for each class member.

Form groups of four or fewer. Give each person a pencil and a copy of the "What Do You See?" handout.

Say: **We're going to do an inkblot test. Look at the**

handout and describe under each inkblot what you see in it. **Don't talk with anyone else about what you see.**

After about two minutes, have people share with their group members what they saw in each of the four pictures.

Then ask the following questions. Allow time for discussion after each question, then have volunteers share their groups' insights with the whole class. Ask:

● **How did you react when you heard how others interpreted the inkblots?** (I was shocked; I felt embarrassed; I knew we'd all see them differently.)

● **What trends, if any, did you discover in the way people interpreted the pictures?** (Some people always saw animals; some people didn't see anything.)

● **How is the diversity of perspectives in this activity like the diversity of perspectives among people?** (Each person sees things a little differently; some people believe that only what they see is right.)

In their groups, have people explain why they saw what they did in the inkblots. Then ask:

● **How did your own view of the inkblots change after hearing the other group members' descriptions?** (I began to see their ideas in the illustration; I saw more than one perspective; it didn't change my perspective at all.)

Say: **Just as each of us may have seen different objects in the inkblots, people we interact with may have different perspectives on Christianity or what it means to be a Christian. Some may have no idea at all what Christianity is, while others may have an inaccurate view. Still others may be searching for truth without really knowing what it looks like. To help us understand what our responsibility is to these various people, let's hear what the Bible has to say.**

Have someone read aloud **Matthew 28:18-20.** Ask:

● **What does this passage tell us about our responsibility as Christians?** (Every Christian is responsible for telling others about Christ; the preachers and teachers are called to spread the gospel.)

● **How does this passage relate to you personally?** (It makes me nervous; I feel honored to be given such a responsibility.)

● **How do the differences we've just talked about relate to how we respond to this passage?** (Some people are gifted in evangelism; they don't—we're all supposed to evangelize; we all share our faith in different ways, depending on our gifts and personalities.)

● **How do people's responses to Christianity differ based on their perspectives?** (People may not understand the message; some may be resistant to Christianity; some may be ready to trust in Jesus.)

BIBLE
I N S I G H T

When Jesus told his disciples to "make disciples," he was telling them to help people become both followers and learners. The noun "disciple" describes a person who seeks knowledge and growth. A disciple isn't content to rest on what he or she knows but wants to better understand the teachings *and* the teacher. This word paints a picture of what God wants from every Christian: a desire to know him better and love him more deeply every day.

Although people sometimes think of the Great Commission as a burden or obligation, it's really a privilege and an honor. God could have spread the gospel in a variety of ways. However, he chose *us.* We alone have the privilege to represent God before others.

THE POINT▷

● **How can we vary the way we share our faith to best utilize our own gifts and people's varying perspectives?** (We can use methods we're most comfortable with; we can meet people at their own levels of understanding; we can be witnesses in whatever way seems natural for us.)

Say: **Because we're all different and every non-Christian's needs and perspectives are different, we must use different methods to tell people about our faith. That's where the diversity of our own gifts and abilities becomes an asset, for▷ we can use our unique gifts and abilities to help others learn about Jesus.**

■■■■■■■■■■■■■■■■■■■■■■■■■■■

FOR *Even Deeper*
DISCUSSION

Form groups of four or fewer and discuss the following questions:

● What's the typical Christian's responsibility in making disciples, baptizing them, and teaching them to obey God? How does a minister's responsibility for these tasks differ from that of the typical Christian? Explain.

● What does Jesus mean in Matthew 28:20 when he says he'll be with us always? Is he with us in a special way when we're telling others about him? Explain.

■■■■■■■■■■■■■■■■■■■■■■■■■■■

□ OPTION 2:
Finding Your Comfort Zone

(25 to 35 minutes)

Before class, make one copy of the "Everyday Evangelists" handout (p. 61) for each person. At one end of the room, tape a sheet of paper with "1" written on it. Tape another sheet of paper with "2" on it at the other end of the room.

Say: **I'm going to read aloud a series of statements. After I read each pair of statements, stand by the number representing the statement that best describes you. After you choose where you'll stand, quickly find a partner and tell that person why this statement describes you better than the other. In this activity, there are no right or wrong responses.**

Read the following statements, allowing approximately one minute between each pair of statements for participants to discuss why they chose that statement. Say:

**If you consider yourself an extrovert, stand by #1.
If you consider yourself an introvert, stand by #2.**

If you enjoy helping other people through your actions, stand by #1.

If you enjoy helping other people through teaching or talking, stand by #2.

If you're somewhat afraid of telling someone about your faith, stand by #1.

If you're invigorated by the idea of telling someone about your faith, stand by #2.

If you relate well with children, stand by #1.

If you relate better with other adults, stand by #2.

If you're more like a soldier, stand by #1.

If you're more like a doctor, stand by #2.

After people discuss the final pair of statements, have them form groups of four or fewer, with at least one "soldier" and one "doctor" in each group. Instruct groups to discuss the following questions, beginning with a soldier in each group. After each question, ask volunteers to share insights with the rest of the class. Ask:

● **What conclusions can you draw from this exercise?** (This is a diverse group of people; we have a lot in common.)

● **What trends, if any, did you discover from this activity?** (All the extroverts enjoy public speaking; most of the extroverts considered themselves to be soldiers.)

Say: **This activity gives us a glimpse into the diversity of abilities and gifts in this group. Now we're going to see how that diversity relates to the types of evangelists we can become.**

Give each person a photocopy of the "Everyday Evangelists" handout and a pencil. Say: **Complete your handout to find out what kind of everyday evangelist you're most like. Then discuss the questions at the bottom of the handout with your group members.**

Allow 10 to 15 minutes for people to complete the handout and discuss the questions. Then ask people to share insights from their groups with the rest of the class.

Say: **Each method of telling someone about Christ is valid. Whether you're a Public Preacher or a Subtle Servant,** ▷ **your unique gifts and abilities can help fulfill the Great Commission.**

◁ **T H E   P O I N T**

Instruct people to tell their group members what they most appreciate about their styles of everyday evangelism. For example, someone might tell a Public Preacher that he or she appreciates the boldness of that person's witness, or someone might tell a Subtle Servant how much he or she appreciates the time that person spends helping others.

■■■■■■■■■■■■■■■■■■■■■■■■■■■■■■■

FOR *Even Deeper* **DISCUSSION** Form groups of four or fewer and discuss the following questions:

● According to Ephesians 4:7-11, some Christians have the gift of evangelism. How does having (or not having) that spiritual gift relate to a Christian's responsibility to share his or her faith?

● Is witnessing through one's lifestyle without talking about Jesus a sufficient way to share the Christian faith? Explain.

● Think about the principle of telling others about Jesus through your gifts and abilities. Who can you think of who does that well? What makes him or her effective? What can you learn from that person about sharing your faith?

■■■■■■■■■■■■■■■■■■■■■■■■■■■■■■■

APPLY■IT■TO **LIFE** **THIS WEEK** The "Apply-It-To-Life This Week" handout (p. 62) helps people further explore the issues uncovered in today's class. Give everyone a photocopy of the handout. Encourage class members to take time during the coming week to explore the questions and activities listed on the handout.

CLOSING

God Be With Us

(up to 10 minutes)

Instruct adults to form groups of four or fewer. If you used the "Finding Your Comfort Zone" activity, make sure each group includes representatives of at least two types of everyday evangelists (based on the "Everyday Evangelists" handout). If you didn't use the "Finding Your Comfort Zone" activity, give everyone a sheet of paper and a pencil.

Tell group members to determine ways they'll support each other's everyday evangelism during the coming weeks. Have each group member identify (but not name) one to three individuals or groups of people he or she would like to tell about Jesus. Then ask group members to create a support plan that specifies how long group members will be committed to praying for each other, when (and if) they'll meet together, and what they'll do to encourage each other to share their faith. Encourage people to be accountable to their group members during the agreed-upon time. Tell class members to write their plans on their papers or on the backs of their "Everyday Evangelists" handouts.

Say: **Write down your group members' names and phone numbers and do your best to support each other as you've planned. Together,▷ with our unique abilities and gifts, we can help fulfill our mission to teach all the nations about Jesus.**

◁ THE POINT

Form a circle, have people join hands, and lead the class in a closing prayer. Begin the prayer by saying: **Dear God, thank you for helping us discover our unique ways of sharing your message with others. Help us be everyday evangelists in all situations and with all people. Help us as we reach out . . .**

Ask adults to continue the prayer by calling out times they'll reach out to others with God's love or people they'll reach out to. For example, someone might continue the prayer by saying "to my co-workers," "when I'm visiting my relatives," or "when someone asks me what I believe." Close the prayer by saying "amen," then thank everyone for participating in the course.

Ask people what they liked most about the course as well as what they'd like to see changed. Please note their comments (along with your own) and send them to the Adult Curriculum Editor at Group Publishing, Inc., Box 481, Loveland, Colorado 80539. We want your feedback so we can make each course better than the last. Thanks!

 For Extra Time

COURSE REFLECTION
(up to 5 minutes)

Ask class members to reflect on the past four lessons. Have them take turns completing the following sentences:
- Something I learned in this course was . . .
- If I could tell friends about this course, I'd say . . .
- Something I'll do differently because of this course is . . .

FOLLOW ME
(up to 10 minutes)

Form groups of four or fewer. Instruct group members to read two passages related to Jesus' calling of his disciples: Matthew 4:18-25 and 9:9-13. Then ask groups to discuss the following questions.
- How did Jesus get people to follow him?
- What methods of evangelism do we see in these passages?
- What did Jesus do to attract disciples that we are unable to do?
- What did Jesus do to attract disciples that we *can* do?

What Do You See?

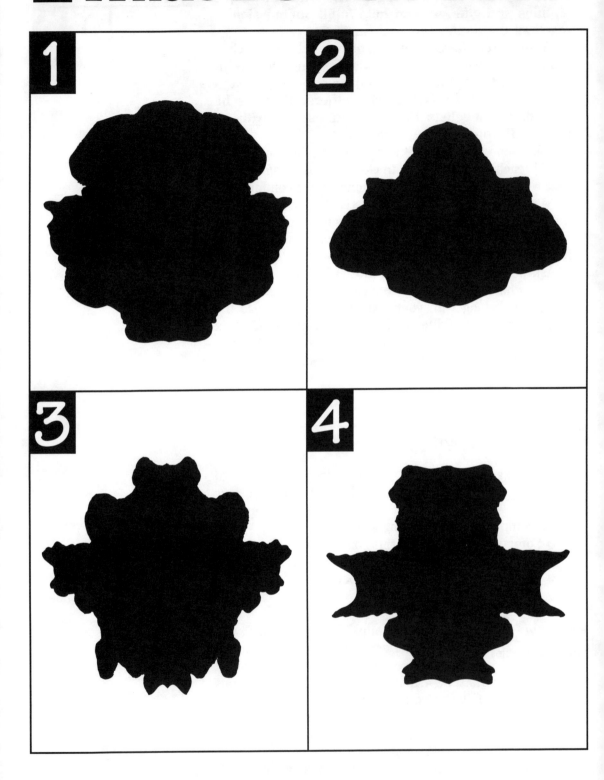

Permission to photocopy this handout from Group's Apply-It-To-Life™ Adult Bible Curriculum granted for local church use.
Copyright © Group Publishing, Inc., Box 481, Loveland, CO 80539.

EVERYDAY EVANGELISTS

Use this handout to determine how you can best use your gifts to share God's love with others.

1. Read the descriptions below and determine which best fits your style of sharing Jesus with others. It's likely that you fit more than one category, but determine which describes you most accurately, then mark only one box.

☐ **Ready Responder:** You enjoy one-on-one interaction about faith issues. You don't feel comfortable in front of a classroom of people, but you're comfortable sharing Scripture truths with someone who's approached you about your faith.

☐ **Subtle Servant:** While you don't feel very comfortable talking about your faith, you practice it daily by opening your house to others, reaching out to those in need, and trying to live a Christlike life. You're the first one in line to prepare a meal for someone in need, but you have a hard time speaking to others about what Jesus can do for them.

☐ **Public Preacher:** You're comfortable talking about your faith in front of people. You may not be an actual preacher, but you can thoughtfully and enthusiastically talk about the Christian faith. You believe your strength is understanding the Scriptures and helping people discover how the Bible applies to their lives.

☐ **Affirming Anchor:** You spend much of your time supporting fellow Christians in their efforts. You don't feel called to preach to non-Christians; rather, you want to serve those who do. You're a born affirmer and love to encourage others.

☐ **Opportunity Knocker:** You don't feel comfortable bringing up your faith in conversations with non-Christians, but when an opportunity arises to share your faith with someone, you're not afraid to speak honestly.

☐ **Button Blaster:** You wouldn't be uncomfortable wearing a button or T-shirt proclaiming God's message. You enjoy publicly showing that you trust in Jesus. You invite people to talk with you about what it means to be a Christian.

2. Once you've determined which type of everyday evangelist you're most like, read 2 Timothy 1:5-11 and 1 Peter 4:7-11 to see what Paul and Peter have to say to you about using your gifts.

Then discuss the following questions in your group:
● What gifts listed in Romans 12:3-8 and 1 Peter 4:7-11 match the various types of everyday evangelists listed on this handout?
● What do Paul and Peter have to say about using your gifts to proclaim God's truth?
● How does each style of everyday evangelism help people know Christ?
● How do the various types of everyday evangelism complement and support each other?
● Which everyday-evangelist traits would you like to develop further? How will you develop those traits?

Permission to photocopy this handout from Group's Apply-It-To-Life™ Adult Bible Curriculum granted for local church use.
Copyright © Group Publishing, Inc., Box 481, Loveland, CO 80539.

Gifted to Tell

APPLY■IT■TO
THIS WEEK

The Point: ▶ We can use our unique gifts and abilities to teach others about Jesus.

Scripture Focus: Matthew 28:18-20; 2 Timothy 1:5-11; and 1 Peter 4:7-11

Reflecting on God's Word

Each day this week, read one of the following Scriptures and think about how it applies to your style of sharing the gospel. List your discoveries in the space under each passage.

Day 1: 2 Timothy 1:7-8. God gives us a spirit of power.

Day 2: Matthew 8:26. Jesus rebukes the storm and his disciples.

Day 3: Proverbs 3:5-6. We're to trust in the Lord.

Day 4: Matthew 5:38-45. Jesus tells us to love our enemies.

Day 5: 1 Peter 3:15-16. Peter tells us to be ready to share our faith.

Day 6: 1 John 3:17. We show our love through our actions.

Beyond Reflection

1. Invite a minister or an evangelist out to eat and to discuss personal evangelism. Ask for help in areas in which you feel weak. Be open to suggestions on how God might better use your gifts and abilities in spreading his message to others. Offer encouragement for what that person is doing to tell others about Jesus.

2. Plan to meet informally with members of this course a month or so after it's completed. Over coffee, discuss how things have changed in your everyday evangelism since the end of the course. Use this time to offer praise for positive things that have happened and encouragement for the days ahead.

Permission to photocopy this handout from Group's Apply-It-To-Life™ Adult Bible Curriculum granted for local church use.
Copyright © Group Publishing, Inc., Box 481, Loveland, CO 80539.

Fellowship and Outreach Specials

Use the following activities any time you want. You can use them as part of (or in place of) your regular class activities, or you might consider planning a special event based on one or more of the ideas.

Free Food, No Pulpit Pounding

Have class members plan a monthly barbecue or other meal for community members who have no church affiliation. People will need to prepare fliers announcing the event and perhaps even go door to door inviting people. Clearly identify the meal as a gift to anyone who's interested, with no strings attached.

Don't force people to sit through a sermon. Instead, make the simple point that, like the meal, God's grace is free to anyone who wants it. After the meal, have class members talk with anyone interested in knowing what it means to be a Christian.

Church Visit

If your church is small or of medium size, visit the nearest "mega-church" and examine its methods for reaching out to non-Christians. Talk with a pastor of evangelism about successful techniques for bringing more non-Christians to church. After your visit, discuss ideas for embracing more non-Christians into the fellowship of your church.

Church Questions

Have people create a written survey they can use to interview friends, co-workers, neighbors, or people in the church community. Instruct people to include questions such as

- Do you believe in God? Why or why not?
- What's your perception of the church? the Bible?
- Who is Jesus Christ?
- What must a person do to get to heaven?

After people conduct the survey, have them discuss the responses they received. Evaluate the role and effectiveness of surveys in evangelism.

Good News

Help the class develop a "Good News" newsletter or insert for your church bulletin. The newsletter might include columns such as "Creative Ways to Share Your Faith at Work," "How to Reach out to Someone in Need," and "Prayer Concerns." For added benefit, have a pastor or another qualified individual write a regular column on the basics of the Christian faith.

Altar Calls

Form a task force to explore how churches in your community approach the concept of "altar calls" (direct invitations generally given at the end of a church service, encouraging people to make a commitment to Christ). Then invite class members to a potluck dinner or party at which the task force can report what it's discovered. After task force members present their findings and discuss their implications for your church, ask for people's opinions on questions such as

● When, if ever, does an altar call become manipulative?
● Can the Holy Spirit work through the altar call experience? If so, how?
● How often, if ever, should a church give an altar call?

Real Service

Have class members demonstrate their faith by volunteering to help the people of your community. Check with local social service agencies to identify the programs with the greatest needs. Challenge people to stretch themselves and serve sacrificially in one of these programs. Meet periodically so people can report what they've been doing and learn from one another's experiences.